Superstars of the MIAMI HEAT

by Max Hammer

amicus
high interest

Amicus High Interest is published by Amicus
P.O. Box 1329, Mankato, MN 56002
www.amicuspublishing.us

Library of Congress Cataloging-in-Publication Data
Hammer, Max.
  Superstars of the Miami Heat / by Max Hammer.
     pages cm. -- (Pro sports superstars (NBA))
  Includes index.
  ISBN 978-1-60753-770-0 (library binding)
  ISBN 978-1-60753-869-1 (ebook)
  1. Miami Heat (Basketball team)--History--Juvenile literature. 2.
Basketball players--United States--Biography--Juvenile literature. I. Title.
  GV885.52.M53H36 2015
  796.323'6409759381--dc23
                          2014045262

Photo Credits: Lynne Sladky/AP Images, cover, 5; Tom DiPace/AP Images,
2, 18–19; Andrew D. Bernstein/NBAE/Getty Images, 6, 9, 22; Amy E. Conn/
AP Images, 10; Wilfredo Lee/AP Images, 13; Kimberly White/Reuters/
Corbis, 14; Eric Gay/AP Images, 17; Matt York/AP Images, 21

Produced for Amicus by The Peterson Publishing Company
and Red Line Editorial.

Designer Becky Daum
Printed in Malaysia

10 9 8 7 6 5 4 3 2 1

TABLE OF CONTENTS

MEET THE MIAMI HEAT

The Heat play in Miami, Florida. The team started in 1988. They have won three **NBA titles**. The Heat have had many great players. Here are some of the best.

ANDERSEN 11

MIAMI 22

GIBSON 22

5

GLEN RICE

Glen Rice joined the Heat in 1989. He had great shooting skills. He made many three-point shots. Rice once scored 56 points in a game.

ALONZO MOURNING

Alonzo Mourning is tall. He could jump high. That helped him **block** shots. He led the NBA in blocks in 1998.

TIM HARDAWAY

Tim Hardaway was a great passer. He helped teammates score baskets. But Hardaway could score, too. He made flashy plays. He played for the Heat until 2001.

Hardaway's son Tim Jr. plays for the New York Knicks.

UDONIS HASLEM

Udonis Haslem is a hard worker. He is a steady player. He is a tough defender. He gets a lot of **rebounds**. Haslem helped the Heat win three NBA titles. The first was in 2006.

Haslem played in France before joining the Heat.

SHAQUILLE O'NEAL

Shaquille O'Neal is huge. He forced his way to the hoop. He made easy baskets. O'Neal helped Miami win the 2006 title.

O'Neal wore size 23 shoes.

DWYANE WADE

Dwyane Wade has quick moves. He makes great shots. Wade plays well in tough games. He helped the Heat win three titles.

Wade was the NBA Finals MVP in 2006.

LeBRON JAMES

LeBron James first played for the Cleveland Cavaliers. He left to join the Heat in 2010. James is tall and strong. He is also quick. He can stop anybody on defense. James led the Heat to two NBA titles. He went back to the Cavaliers in 2014.

CHRIS BOSH

Chris Bosh joined the Heat in 2010.
He has great skills near the basket.
He can shoot from long range, too.
Bosh helped Miami win two titles.
They were in 2012 and 2013.

The Heat have had many great superstars. Who will be next?

TEAM FAST FACTS

Founded: 1988

Home Arena: American Airlines Arena in Miami, Florida

Mascot: Burnie the Fireball

Leading Scorer: Dwyane Wade (18,280 points as of February 25, 2015)

NBA Championships: 3 (2006, 2012, 2013)

Hall of Fame Players: 2, including Alonzo Mourning

WORDS TO KNOW

block – to stop a ball from going in the basket

MVP – Most Valuable Player; an honor given to the best player in the NBA each season

NBA– the National Basketball Association

NBA Finals – the games played to decide the NBA championship

rebound – a ball that bounces away from the basket after a missed shot

title – an NBA championship victory

LEARN MORE

Books

Frederick, Shane. *The Story of the Miami Heat*.
Mankato, Minn.: Creative Education, 2014.

Savage, Jeff. *Dwyane Wade*. Minneapolis, Minn.: Lerner
Publications Company, 2015.

Websites

Miami Heat History
http://www.nba.com/heat/history
Get more information about the Heat.

NBA History
http://www.nba.com
Learn more about the history of every NBA team.

Sports Illustrated for Kids
http://www.sikids.com
Play games and read about sports.

INDEX